Overcoming Rejection

Rejection From A Crush, An Ex And Also Rejection From Work

(Ultimate Guide For Overcoming Self-doubt, Low Self-esteem And Living With Passion)

Andries Sumpter

Published By **Darby Connor**

Andries Sumpter

Overcoming Rejection: Rejection From A Crush, An Ex And Also Rejection From Work (Ultimate Guide For Overcoming Self-doubt, Low Self-esteem And Living With Passion)

ISBN 978-1-77485-898-1

No part of this guidebook shall be reproduced in any form without permission in writing from the publisher except in the case of brief quotations embodied in critical articles or reviews.

Legal & Disclaimer

The information contained in this ebook is not designed to replace or take the place of any form of medicine or professional medical advice. The information in this ebook has been provided for educational & entertainment purposes only.

The information contained in this book has been compiled from sources deemed reliable, and it is accurate to the best of the Author's knowledge; however, the Author cannot guarantee its accuracy and validity and cannot be held liable for any errors or omissions. Changes are periodically made to this book. You must consult your doctor or get professional medical advice before using any of the suggested remedies, techniques, or information in this book.

Upon using the information contained in this book, you agree to hold harmless the Author from and against any damages, costs, and expenses, including any legal fees potentially resulting from the application of any of the information provided by this guide. This disclaimer applies to any damages or injury caused by the use and application, whether directly or indirectly, of any advice or information presented, whether for breach of contract, tort, negligence, personal injury, criminal intent, or under any other cause of action.

You agree to accept all risks of using the information presented inside this book. You need to consult a professional medical practitioner in order to ensure you are both able and healthy enough to participate in this program.

Table Of Contents

Chapter 1: What Makes A True Friend

After we've identified what rejection looks like and how we can determine if we're being rejected, it's time to identify who we can speak to about being rejected. It is important to be able and willing to make choices about your friends and those you surround you with. By doing this, you won't be led away by people who want to retaliate against people who reject them for whatever reason.

There are some things that you must remember when searching for people who will talk about your rejection. These are the traits that you should be looking for in friends who will always stand beside you, no matter what.

What makes a true friend?"

A friend can be someone you can trust no matter what. Someone who doesn't judge you for whatever you do. These are people you can trust for support no matter how difficult and who will always be there for your back when you need it.

Some people see their family members, especially their siblings, as the first person they can call for help. This should happen. Talking with your family about the events in your life is a good idea. When you can communicate with your family openly, you'll be able find the best way to deal with rejection.

But if you don't feel this way, you should look for someone who you can confide in. Someone who will not judge you if you're weak and fragile.

Someone who will always be there to help you when you need it. If you find someone who is willing to do this for your without hesitation, you'll have the best friend.

Additional Reminders

You can use your friend as a listener to your problems, but it's not a good idea. It is acceptable to use your friend as a sounding board for your problems, but you should also consider his or her feelings. Rejection doesn't automatically mean you have the right to expect others to help you. After you've let go of your thoughts and feelings, it's time to learn how to use them to help you decide what the next step should be. This is what the professionals call "processing".

People who are not able to talk with family or friends can consult professional psychologists, counselors or psychoanalysts to help them cope with the rejection. This allows them to get their thoughts out more efficiently and helps them plan for the future.

To counter the negative emotions that can damage you from the inside and make you stronger through rejection, it is crucial to have a support system. However, it is important to select your friends well.

To Drink or Not Drink

When to seek medical help

It is possible that you do not have any way to release the negative emotions you feel about the rejection. This can make it difficult to handle the situation effectively. In this case, it is important to seek professional help. These are some signs and symptoms to help you know if medical aid is necessary when handling rejection.

When you become emotionally attached to the situation, this is the first sign you aren't capable of handling rejection. If you were mature, you would be able to see the larger picture. You should be able and willing to listen to the other person. You will be able to understand the other person's point of view and you will be able to manage your emotions more effectively to control them faster.

If you withdraw from society, it is not possible to cope well with rejection. You refuse to communicate with others. Even your family. Some individuals will even lock themselves in their rooms and keep them there for long periods. If this is you, you may need to think about your medical options more seriously.

Additionally, obsessive thinking can lead to a tendency to be too focused on the situation. You are not capable of handling rejection alone if you think about it so much that you end up in your own way.

Who can I call?

It is possible that this is the case. If speaking to someone you trust about your situation is not helpful, it is time to consult a professional. Here are some people you might be able talk to that can help you resolve the situation.

* Guidance counsellors

* Psychologists

* Psychiatrists

These people will most likely be able to help and guide you through the situation. They may also offer you medication options that can help clear your mind. This can stop you from regretting doing something that is not right for you.

Significant Reminders

Remember that only psychiatrists can issue medication prescriptions. Guidance counsellors, psychologists, and other mental health professionals are there to help you assess your situation and offer advice. They may be able offer advice and suggestions on other tools you can use to accept rejection sooner rather than later.

But, if you are not ready to seek medical attention, continue reading to find out about alternative methods to dealing with rejection. Although you may not be at the top of your depression yet, you might still be able get out of this negative situation on your own.

To be able communicate with others about your situation and help them to better understand it is the key. If you can talk about it, you'll be well on your path to being a mature and accepting person who can face rejection with a smile.

Chapter 2: Understanding Anxiety

For someone with anxiety, life can be very unpleasant. While everyone else seems to be going through life and enjoying the moment, you feel like you are on the other side, looking at the glass and waiting.

A lot of people accept that anxiety can be a part of everyday life. Most people have learned how to deal with anxiety and it doesn't affect their daily lives. We are talking about anxiety that is persistent, overwhelming, or uncontrollable.

Self-doubt is the most difficult part of anxiety. The worst part about anxiety is the self-doubt. Even your family members may not understand your behavior, or be downright judgmental about your condition. People who don't fully understand anxiety can mistakenly see it as shyness or stress. They simply don't get how overwhelming, discomfiting or all-consuming anxiety can make them feel.

These are the times when those closest to you start to become impatient and tell your to "Pull yourself up" as if you are being selfish. People begin to believe you are trying too hard to avoid them. However, inside you are screaming in terror and pain.

You only need someone who understands you, so you can share your feelings of helplessness or hopelessness with them. This will let you know that you aren't losing your mind and that the thoughts in you mind are normal.

I am sorry if you have this experience. You are not crazy. Anxiety disorder is a very common condition.

What is anxiety?

Anxiety is a medical condition where there is excessive and unreasonable fear of normal situations. Anxiety can cause you to be unable or unwilling to participate in daily activities. This disorder is severe and requires treatment as with any other normal physical condition.

But, most Americans don't realize that anxiety disorders are the most widespread disorders in the USA. The sad truth is that 13 million Americans who are suffering from anxiety disorders do not receive treatment. This means that more than 40million people, both men and women, suffer from them. This shows that it is very common.

An anxiety disorder is simply a general term. Anxiety disorders include panic attacks, generalized anxious disorder (GAD), anxiety disorder with social anxiety, and phobias.

Do you think it's anxiety or stress?

A lot of people confuse normal anxiety with anxiety disorder. They are completely distinct. These are just a handful of examples to help you see the difference.

* Stress causes you to worry about bills, losing your job, or being dumped by your girlfriend. The trigger or stressor must be removed before you can worry about anything. An anxiety disorder makes you constantly worry about these things, even if it is not. You may experience daily distress, even though the stressor has gone.

* Stress is when you go to a social occasion and feel self-conscious or uncomfortable. This could be due to the way you dress. An anxiety disorder causes you to avoid social gatherings because you fear that you will be embarrassed.

* Stress is how you feel before you take an exam, present a paper, or go to an interview. A stressor can be a significant

event that has a negative impact on your life. Anxiety disorder is a situation in which you feel a sudden, overwhelming fear without any reason. You live in constant fear of experiencing another panic attack.

* Stress can be defined as a rational fear of something you perceive to be dangerous, such as a place, person or object. After you get rid of the dangerous object or the place, you'll be fine. An anxiety disorder causes you to fear non-threatening things. You can still be very afraid even if the object is removed.

* Stress refers to the immediate reaction you have after a traumatic experience, such as when you are able to avoid a collision with a car. This situation can make it difficult to sleep. An anxiety disorder is a condition where you have frequent flashbacks or nightmares from the accident that occur months, or even years, after it happened.

Researchers continue to discover more about anxiety disorders. They discovered that anxiety disorders can run in families, and they have a biological basis. Our understanding is that anxiety disorders result from a complex mix risk factors. These include genetics and personality.

Anxiety in different forms

There are many different types of anxiety disorder. We'll be focusing our attention on three: panic attacks, anxiety disorder, and social anxiety disorder.

Social Anxiety Disorders

Social anxiety is defined as an intense fear of being judged and scrutinized by others in social situations. This is an anxiety disorder that can cause extreme self-consciousness even in normal social settings. You feel embarrassed by what you do publicly because everyone around you is always watching.

Social anxiety is also known as socialphobia. It usually begins before age 18 and can affect work or school. People suffering from this disorder know they have excessive fear of social situations, but they don't know how. A person with this disorder may spend weeks or days worrying about an upcoming event. This can lead to depression and low self esteem. Although it's easy for people to assume they are shy, shyness is not the same as social anxiety.

Particular situations, like those that require public speaking or performing in public, can trigger social anxiety. It can be very difficult and embarrassing to maintain any type of romantic or social relationship. It is only natural to feel comfortable with family members.

The symptoms

The following symptoms are physical signs of social anxiety:

* Increased sweating

Blushing

  * Restrictive posture

  * Rapid pulse

  * Speak too quietly

  * Trembling

  * Nausea

  * Difficulty speaking

  * Mild stomach cramps

  * Refusing eye contact

These symptoms can cause you to feel more self-conscious. This creates a vicious cycle.

Causes

The amygdala is a tiny part in your brain that causes social anxiety. This research continues. This structure controls fear responses. It is also possible to pass on your social anxiety to your children. Hormones and trauma from childhood are other risk factors.

Treatment

If you seek the advice of a medical professional, social anxiety can often be managed. There are many treatments available. However, the most effective is cognitive-behavioral (CBT), and certain medications. CBT, which exposes you to the things that make you fearful, is the best treatment. CBT involves exposing you to the situation or object which makes you anxious. Then, you learn to manage the criticism or rejection you normally dislike. We will cover this in more detail in one chapter.

Panic Attacks

A panic attack refers to a sudden onset and rapid increase in fear over a short period of time. Although panic attacks are characterized by overwhelming fear and anxiety, you may not fully understand what's happening.

Because of the increased heart rate and other intense symptoms, it feels as though you are in imminent danger of having a heart attack. But, the psychological factors that are causing your panic attack may also be contributing to it. A panic attack lasts between 15 and 20 seconds. You should just let it go and wait for your body's return to normal.

While panic attacks might seem uncommon, they are fairly common. Panic attacks are more common in women than in men. It is possible to have panic attacks at any age. However, the majority of people experience the symptoms between 25-30 years of age.

The symptoms

If you want to be diagnosed as suffering from panic attacks, you need to experience at least four of these symptoms:

* Sweating

* Heart palpitations, an increase in heart rate

* Trembling

* Shortness in breath

* Choking sensations

* Chest pain

* Feeling cold/hot

* Light-headedness

* Abdominal discomfort

* Feeling overwhelmed by life?

* Fear of the dying

* Tingling, numb sensations

Causes

The adrenaline hormone floods the body from fear, which is what causes panic attacks. Notice the word "perceived" in this sentence. It means that the problem you are experiencing is psychological. These symptoms will appear as you increase your adrenaline level. But, it is unlikely that the hormone will remain at such a high level for too long.

Your panic attacks could also be caused by stress, too much coffee or insufficient sleep. The best thing to do is try to identify the cause of the attack. You might have received bad news about your loved one's health or an impending exam. An understanding of the cause can help you avoid panic attacks and decrease anxiety.

Treatment

There are many options to help you manage panic attacks symptoms. These solutions include taking slow deep breaths, listening to music or watching TV, breathing into a paper bag or keeping your eyes open. Deep breathing, mindfulness or progressive muscle relaxation are all options for relaxation. Psychological treatment often involves cognitive-behavioral therapies. We will discuss some of these treatment options more in the coming chapters.

Although some people have only one or two attacks per year, others may experience recurrences. You should get a physical exam to find out what the problem might be. If you ignore the problem, you could end up with panic attacks or a panic disorder. You may experience panic disorder if you have panic attacks that are repeated each month. Then you might become paranoid about getting more. Agonyphobia is a fear of wide open spaces and places that don't offer an escape route.

Phobias

A phobia refers to a severe fear that is irrational of an object or situation, even though it is not a threat. Let's assume you live in an apartment building with 20 floors. However, you fear falling from the building. You may be scared of a tiny spider you don't know is poisonous. But you panic and get anxious when you do. These are examples phobias.

Phobias, which are quite common for most people is nothing to be ashamed of. If the fear is persistent for more than six month and keeps you from living your normal life, it could be a psychological problem. If you've lived in your 20-story apartment for more than six months and are still afraid of falling from the balcony, then you may have a phobia.

The symptoms

Phobias result in severe fear when you are exposed to an object, or encounter a specific situation. Some objects can cause physical symptoms just by the thought of them.

* Lightheadedness

* Choking sensation

* Trembling

* Cold and hot flushes

* Vomiting

* Accelerated pulse pace

* Sweating

* Numberness

* Shortness in breath

* Tight sensation in the chest

* Feeling completely detached from your body

These are signs that you might have a panic attack or phobia. There are also times when the symptoms may get severe and cause panic attacks. A panic attack can make you embarrassed and withdraw from social situations where you may be confronted with your fear. While avoidance is one strategy to deal with fear, it will only make the fear worse. It will also negatively impact your daily life.

Types and types of phobias

Phobias may be divided into:

1.Specific phobias: This is where you're afraid of one thing. They can start as children but they fade as you grow older.

2.Complex Phobias- These are far more serious than specific phobias. Because they occur in your adult life, they disrupt your normal functioning. They fall under the categories of social phobias or agoraphobia. Both have been covered before.

Causes

Research suggests that your phobia isn't caused by one factor. There could be many factors that are responsible. They include:

* Specific trauma-Extreme turbulence or a flight that was too turbulent during childhood might cause fear of flying.

* Childhood environment: Your parents may have been constantly anxious or overly fearful in childhood, and you were taught to respond in that way.

* Genetics

* Long-term stress

* Panic reactions

Treatment

Identify the root cause of your phobia and take action to address them. You can seek professional assistance and follow the recommended methods to deal with your phobia. Cognitive-behavioral Therapy is often used by professionals to help with phobia management. It is possible to relax using relaxation techniques like controlled breathing and stretching. A good option is to practice mindfulness. These techniques are described in detail in the chapters that follow.

Joining a support group is another option. This allows you to meet other sufferers, share your experiences, and learn coping techniques. These support groups are available online and in person.

Chapter 3: Overcoming Fears And Anxiety

There are several techniques that can really help with anxiety and fear. Some people may have phobias. However, this chapter is not about that. It is about social anxiety and fear, which many people who are depressed have difficulty dealing with. This chapter will teach you how to build confidence and overcome social fears.

Exercise 6 - Learning relaxation methods

These relaxation methods are helpful in difficult situations. Depressed people may feel anxious in new situations. It could be related to any medication you are taking. If you're in a safe environment, you won't have this problem. If you attempt to meet people or experience something new, you may panic.

There are many ways to handle panic, but one of my favorite ways is to learn how to relax. It relaxes the mind, makes it more open to new possibilities and allows you to be more open to them. You can't have enough peace if your mind is filled with black thoughts or retrospective thoughts. It's this inner peace that will help you overcome the terrible feelings you feel when faced with a social situation.

Find a quiet place where you are free from interruptions. To make sure you feel comfortable, place your back on the ground and support your head. You don't need to wear restrictive clothing. Close your eyes, and visualize every part of the body. Tendonize your toes and watch them relax. Take a deep look at that particular part of your body while you inhale through the nose and exhale through the mouth. Continue doing this to other parts of your body until relaxation is achieved.

The exercise helps you improve your control of your breathing and to energize yourself. This is essential for social interaction.

Panic Attack

This makes you feel insecure and socially unworthy. Your mind becomes panicky and you want to escape the circumstances that led to it. This exercise helps you breathe better and prevents you from feeling panicky.

Exercise 7 - Breathing

You have to learn how to calm down when panic sets in. It's common for people to use a paper bag to inhale, but it can be difficult when you're out. If you are able to find quiet, you can perform breathing exercises that help to restore the oxygen in your body and lift you from panic.

Close your eyes. You will need to breathe in through your nose for 8 counts. Continue to hold that air for a few moments. After that, you can exhale through your mouth until the count is 12. Continue to exhale through the mouth until you reach 12. You can continue this exercise by being aware of the air entering your nose and leaving your body. Take a moment to notice your breaths. Only think about your breath.

This exercise is designed to drain excess energy from the body caused by poor breathing. It helps you calm down when you are in panic.

If you have anxiety or panic attacks, both of these exercises will help. You'll feel more comfortable and relaxed when you do these exercises. They might even save the day. Because the sitting up breathing exercise can easily be done wherever you happen to be. If you're in a quiet area, you can also do it privately.

You can do it slowly. If you don't have the experience of socializing for a while, it is unlikely that you will be able to quickly become a social butterfly. Instead of trying to get out of your shell and trying to make friends quickly, you should be willing to let people know about you and support yourself.

Chapter 4: How To Handle Rejection

Because rejection can sometimes seem like a personal attack and is difficult to handle, disassociation is often the best approach. It is easy to get wrapped up in the idea that rejection is a personal attack.

It is possible to address rejection through a simple step-by–step process. This allows us to deal with our emotions and addresses our deepest fears. But before you look at the process, consider yourself. You must address your You-centric issues before you can dig deeper into the subconscious. You are probably familiar with the feelings of rejection and have dealt or are dealing. But, have you ever stopped and thought about why this is happening?

It may seem complex, but it isn't. Try to find the root cause of your rejection and use logical reasoning to help you. Do you behave rationally? Does your behavior make sense? Does your behavior make sense?

This process of isolating the source is often referred by trained professionals. A primary source can look like a bad Apple. You only get to the inside when you cut it open. This kind of dissection serves two purposes. First, it helps you address the problem that you previously didn't see. Second, you can also learn that this enemy isn't new to you. You have already won and fought this battle before, even if you only knew it sub-consciously.

Once you've completed this step, you can now come to terms. Recognize that rejections may not be just about you. Many rejections are caused by self-doubt and insecurity. This does not mean, however, that the rejection is not your fault. It is likely that something you have said or done may have been a factor in the rejection. By being open with yourself and able to move on with your life, you will be able to improve upon who you are.

Chapter 5: How Do You Handle Being Dumped?

It can be devastating to have someone you love break up with you, especially if it comes out of the blue. Although it is rare for a breakup to happen out of the blue in reality, it does not always happen.

You will feel awful. Shock will become disbelief. And when it sinks in, symptoms can include shaking, guilt or rage, the desire to fall over and die, and even physical sickness. Jilted lovers may vomit or develop flu-like symptoms in some cases.

It depends on how emotional you put into your relationship (real, imagined), it can take as little as one week for your physical symptoms to resolve. If your symptoms don't resolve in a week or less, it is time to seek professional assistance.

It won't be easy to overcome emotional trauma even if you try. Depression, mental dullness or lack of energy can all last several months. This is when you may be tempted to revisit old haunts and pore over photos. You might also want to listen to the same music as your loved ones.

Although it may seem difficult, most people agree that the best solution to any past mementos, especially pictures, is to just throw them away. These things can only be used to reinforce the sometimes vain hope that there is still a chance of you getting back together.

According to some therapists, most people take between four to six weeks to recover from depression. After that point, there should be periods of improvement. You will experience periods of intense sadness, depending on how emotionally invested you are in your relationship. However, the good days may be interrupted by periods of high spirits. The latter will fade over the next weeks. In some cases, rage may replace the depression. These should, however, pass.

You don't have to isolate yourself after a breakup, but you can speed up your recovery by not being too dependent on yourself. Studies show that people who have a network to share their grief with are more likely to recover from the emotional trauma of being married than those who do it all alone.

The moment you reach closure is when it will be over. This is when it becomes clear that you have lost all emotional connection to the other person. The day comes when, without realizing it, you will hear the same piece of music, but it doesn't cause you to cry anymore.

Do not forget that the maximum period of grieving should be six months. If you continue to feel terrible after that time, you might be suffering from depression. If you are experiencing severe depression, it is time to seek help from a professional.

Research has shown that Tylenol, which is a generic Tylenol, can reduce the pain associated with rejection. The ball-tossing experiment involved having some subjects take Tylenol just before the procedure. The results were surprising: those who did felt less emotional pain as compared to those who didn't.

Tylenol also was used in the study to examine the effects of painful memories upon IQ levels. They found that Tylenol users who received a placebo had lower scores.

This is yet more evidence that our brains do not distinguish between emotional and bodily pain. Many people believe antidepressants are a sign of weakness. However, research has shown that this is no different to asthmatics who must have inhalers.

Chapter 6: Have A Growth Mindset And Feel Confident

Winston Churchill, British writer, politician, and officer in the army, once rightfully stated that.

"Success and failure are not final. Failure is not fatal. It is the determination to go on that counts.

Failure is not fatal and success is not permanent. Fear of failure is what keeps us from moving forward. We have distorted our perceptions about success and failure. That is why it is often difficult to be courageous.

Failure and success are common parts of our lives. These are common experiences that we all have and will continue to experience in different stages of our lives. However, we should not allow them to dictate how we live. You will succeed in some areas of your life and you will fail in others. The success you have should not be able to control or make it too important. In life you will face failure many times. It is important to be resilient and keep trying. In order to achieve your goal, you must have control over your emotions, thoughts and attitude. This is possible if you cultivate a positive, growth-oriented mindset.

How a Growth Mindset Will Make You Courageous

Your mindset is your set of beliefs, ideologies or core values. Your mindset is the summation of all you believe. It sets a clear pattern and guideline that will help you live your life in a certain way. It can be divided broadly into two types, fixed and growth mindset.

A fixed mindset or limiting mindset is composed of different beliefs that remind you of past failures and reinforce your belief that you cannot move beyond a certain point. You believe you can never reach your dreams because your potential limits. This is the mindset that leads to fear and prevents you from achieving your goals.

A growth mindset is the opposite. It helps you realize that success and progress are possible. You are capable of reaching your full potential if you work hard and persevere. To overcome fears, believe in your abilities and be inspired to pursue your dreams and goals with courage, you need these beliefs. It's when you believe that failure doesn't have to be fatal and that it is possible and acceptable to rise from your mistakes that you can keep going and work hard for what you believe.

Here are some tips to help you cultivate a growth mindset.

Gently Calm your Inner Critic to Nurture Positive Self-talk

Your inner critic is the name you use to refer to that annoying voice within you that tells your you are not capable of succeeding, you cannot be successful, it is impossible, too difficult, or you will fail again every time you try something risky, brave, or what brings you pure joy.

This voice is your alter-ego. It's a result years of negative selftalk. Your self talk is what you say about yourself. Negative selftalk is created when you degrade and criticize yourself. Your negative thoughts and beliefs will stick in your mind, and can influence your outlook. By encouraging positive self-talk, you can help to shift your inner critic.

* Be conscious of the voice within you. You can listen to those thoughts when you are working on a goal.

* Note the thought in your journal.

* Repeat the statement loudly, then take a moment to analyze it. Ask yourself how many times you have been laughed at by people because you said, "I fear speaking out in public because people may laugh about my thoughts. That is why I'm not a motivational speaker." If you don't speak publicly, it is possible that this has never happened. If that has ever happened, and someone laughed at your mistakes or stammered, then you can accept that there will always been noise around you.

* This is the time to be kind and grateful to the negative voice in your head. Use phrases like "Thanks for making my fear aware" or "It's OK, it's all fine."

* Next, try to think of something more real and positive. This will help you replace your negative voice. For example, you could say "Oh, it's scary to boldly and confidently address people in public," but you'll eventually find the courage to do so.

If you are feeling upset or troubled by thoughts or emotions, you can start a calming and uplifting dialogue with them. You can gently change the direction of your thoughts to be more positive. You'll soon find a positive attitude and positive self-talk. This will allow you to have faith in yourself and not settle with anything less than what is best for you.

Positive affirmations can be used

A positive affirmation can be a positive suggestion that you repeat to your brain. It will rewire your brain to think positively. This will help you build positive beliefs and attract positive experiences. You will find it easier to act and think positively. It becomes a habit.

Here are some ways to use positive affirmations.

* Create positive affirmations based on your daily objectives and activities. These

affirmations will instill confidence and strength inside you.

* Your affirmation should be brief enough that you can quickly chant. You should limit it to between 5-10 words.

It should be positive and not contain words that have negative connotations like 'never', "not", or the like. These words will not be perceived by your subconscious mind. Your subconscious mind may perceive your suggestion as if you said, "I won't give in my fear," and you'll likely give in.

* It must have a present-oriented orientation. This indicates it is able to tell you that you have achieved your goals. Saying, "I am brave" instead of "I will become courageous" is a good example. However, your subconscious cannot discern between reality or imagination. It will believe what you tell it and give you confidence. If you chant "I want it to be

confident", it will place emphasis on your future and make sure you don't forget it in the present.

* When you have your affirmation in place, say it loudly, slowly, and with firm conviction. You can also write the affirmation as you chant.

* Also, picture yourself experiencing that improvement. You can chant, "I face mine fears courageously", and imagine yourself facing your most difficult fears and conquering them.

* Daily chant positive affirmations to feel more

Here are some confidence-based affirmations t

* I can be confident and face my fears without

* I exhale courage, and I inhale fear.

* I have complete control over my fears, and ca

* I do everything to achieve my goals with cour

* I am happy because my strength makes me ha

You should practice these skills and be kind to others. If you fall short, you still have the ability to get up again and attempt your goals.

You must also learn to accept your fears, work on your weaknesses, and then take the steps necessary to live with courage every single day. The next chapter will provide more details on how to do it.

Chapter 7: Signs That Your Fear Of Failure And Rejection Might Be Present

Individuals can experience psychological tension from fear. This is easily recognized by their signs and symptoms. This is due their behavior in response to anxiety and anticipation.

* "Rejection just motivates to keep trying, and to try harder." Sasha Grey.

* "There are times to speak up about your fears and times to ignore them."

Here are some signs and symptoms to look for.

They are constantly concerned about how others will view their achievement.

People often worry about what the end result might be. They also worry about what others think and what they will do if they fail. They are usually afraid to do badly, because they fear judgement. Their performance is always driven by pleasing others.

Be apprehensive about your future endeavours

If one is afraid, they are more likely to be anxious about the future and to doubt their ability to make the choices that will best suit them. They live in fear and act out their fears. They are constantly troubled by the question "What if"?

They like to regret.

When they fail, they tend to think about what they could have done differently to make it better. They feel guilty about letting an opportunity pass them by.

Always question their intelligence or capability

Many people with a fearful mindset view themselves as weaklings in various areas. They don't believe that they are as qualified or as expected. Fear overtakes their thoughts and clouds them with negativity.

Anticipating bad results

Fearful people always tell people upfront that they don't expect to be successful so as not to lower expectations. They do this in order to avoid disappointments. They have never given up on their ability and will continue to work on their projects.

Reluctantness or unwillingness to try new items

Fear can be a significant hindrance to your willingness to try new things in your life. People who fear taking chances are always afraid. They always see the negative.

Chapter 8: How To Identify Anger, Fear, And Stress

(If you're already suffering from them).

Once you have a basic understanding of these strong emotions, it is time to learn the identifying factors that will help you to address them.

Fear. Fear. Rational fear, or good fear; and irrational fear, or bad fear.

A good or rational fear is the type we normally feel because of an imminent danger or threat to survival or our existence. It is the kind that triggers your instincts telling you what the best action is, the kind that makes your hair stand up, the type which gives you an adrenaline rush and makes you a 15-minute superhero or superwoman. The type that lets your mind pause and review your general knowledge in order to be able address this particular fear. It should be the only kind of fear that you should feel, if possible.

Negativity can also cause irrational fears. It causes anxiety, shortness of breathing, panic attacks, and blood loss to the extremities. Most of the time, it leaves your brain with little blood flow. In extreme cases, it can cause paranoia and phobia.

Anger. Anger is an indication of anger. You might laugh about it, because you may be feeling a type of fear that is not anger. Like I stated in the previous chapters, anger is never without reason. Fear is the root of anger. If fear thrives in your body, it slowly begins to nourish your anger.

It's possible you don't feel it right away so let me show you another. Imagine your most irritating coworker. It's the type of officemate that causes you to laugh but not your eye rolls. It could be that your officemate is a threat, or your career goals, or steals the spotlight. There is a reason for this individual to make eye rolls.

If you suppress anger, an eye roll is a sign that something is wrong. While you could say that this is a baby version of anger at the moment, it can be distracting from the fact that the anger is growing and being nurtured. Other symptoms include jaw-clenching (jaw-clenching), tapping feet, tapping ears, ringing in your stomach, and other behaviors such as fist-clenching. If you spend a little more time fueling the fire, your anger will quickly escalate and you'll soon witness one its most intense forms through your own eyes.

Stress. The three emotions we are discussing are strongly correlated. It is important that you know that anger and stress are often correlated.

Here is a list of characteristics, both physical, psychological, behavior, and emotional that people can experience under stress. These characteristics are due to anger, stress, and fear. It can also cause damage to your body from the inside. It is important to note that stress can cause many different symptoms.

* Physical. These include headaches, stomach problems, constipation and delayed menstruation.

* Psychological. A tendency to be anxious, depressed and distracted, less productive or creative, and lately, to become a worrywart.

* Behavioral. Apathy, forgetfulness and nervousness.

* Emotional. Anger, frustration, anger, or defensive behavior.

Now that you have identified the fundamental characteristics of stress, it doesn't mean you are only feeling one. Instead, you can confidently say that you are experiencing all of them. Take the time to observe and then feel. Once you have felt two or three of these feelings, it is time to take a look back. Do you remember displaying anger in the past? Have you ever displayed anger? If so, take a look at the past. Which reason or fear do you believe is causing your anger? You must think before you jump to conclusions.

Chapter 9: How To Deal With Them

It's amazing! It is now possible to correctly identify the three powerful and notorious emotions. Let's not stop here! Let me tell you how to handle these emotions so that you can let go of their bonds.

Acceptance. First and foremost, it is impossible to address an issue without acceptance. Although we all can accept stress, anger and fear can be difficult to handle.

Some people may be able to admit that they are angry. Others aren't humble enough or brave enough to face their fears. If you're reading this book now, it is likely that you are seeking help. It is okay to be vulnerable and admit to your fears. Anger isn't always without fear. Look within to find the fear. It can be small and silly as well as big and frightening. Let's just take the time to acknowledge them now, and let's get rid it together.

Feel. Accept them. Feel them. Adults often make the common error of suppressing their feelings. You look at a young child. They barely know everything. A child's emotions are very sensitive.

It is false to believe that crying is only for children. This is what we as adults forget. Crying and pouring your heart out. These seem to be signs of weakness. Crying and crying are signs of strength. They show that you can stand up for your feelings even when you live in a shallow, judgmental society. Instead, suppressing anger and hiding fear is what makes you weak.

When they cry, it's over. This is why their lives are so bright and sunny, and ours are so dark and bleak.

It is impossible to control your emotions. Ever. Contrary what popular belief says, emotions are not always easy to control. It is their purpose, and why they exist.

Emotions are not controllable. We must let them be. Don't try to force it.

Chapter 10: How To Deal With Them

It's amazing! It is now possible to correctly identify these strong emotions. We are not done! Let me tell you how to handle these emotions so that you can let go of their bonds.

Acceptance. First and foremost, it is impossible to address an issue without acceptance. Although we all can accept stress, anger and fear are not easy to handle.

Some people may be able to admit that they are angry. Others aren't brave enough to acknowledge their feelings. You're most likely at this point to seek help. It is okay to be vulnerable and admit your fears, but only if you do so honestly. Anger isn't always without fear. Look within to find the fear. It can be small, silly, scary or large. Let's just take the time to acknowledge them now.

Feel. Once you accept them, let them feel. Adults often make the common error of suppressing their feelings. You look at a young child. They barely know everything. A child's emotions are very sensitive.

It is false to believe that crying is only for children. See? That's what we forget as adults. Crying and crying out. We believe these are signs that we are weak. Crying and crying out can be an indicator of strength. It shows that you are strong and will stand up for yourself even when you live in a shallow, judgmental society. Instead, suppressing anger and hiding fear is what makes you weak.

When they cry, It's done. This is why their life seems bright, cheerful and fun. It's what makes our lives as adults so dark and bleak.

It is impossible to control your emotions. Ever. Contrary what popular belief says, emotions are not always easy to control. It is their purpose, and why they exist.

Emotions are not controllable. We must let them be. Don't try to force it.

Release. Imagine your feelings as butterflies. You cannot let go of your feelings if you haven't touched or held them. To feel your emotions is to let the butterfly perch on top of you. Only then will it be possible to let go of your emotions.

It's okay to rant about your feelings in your journal, blog, music, art, or other mediums. You could also ask a friend to read your Ramblings. You can trust a friend to help you release your emotions. No matter how tumultuous your emotions may be, a friend will always help you get out what you need.

Chapter 11: Events Which Trigger Anger

"Holding on anger is like gripping a hot coke with the intent to throw it at another person, except that you are actually the one who gets burned."

Buddha

People rarely get angry unless their brains are in danger. However, anger triggers can differ from person to person. The factors that influence your triggers, in turn, can be affected by:

* Models are role models that can be learned and co

* Recollections and experiences of childhood, includi

* Past history of abuse or neglect

*Poverty/financial difficulty

* Experience and level control and power

If an event triggers your anger, then it's likely that you have experienced something similar in the past. These can be sensitive or intimate areas of your personal life or long-standing, unresolved, or recurring issues.

Anger triggers can be outlined as:

* Congestion or overcrowding, particularly if it is

* Waiting for a doctor to see you. This can be some level of emotional, mental or physical disco

* People who are also agitated can cause conges

* A friend, colleague, or coworker making a joke

* A colleague who arrives at work in a bad mooc

* Being wrongfully indicted.

* A neighbor who plays too loud music. This can easily escalate if the neighbor does not stop playing music, even after numerous attempts to communicate.

* Some smells.

Anger triggers can be described as situations, people or events that "push you buttons".

Self-Assessment Exercise

Create 4 columns on a sheet (or on your computer) and label them with the following:

Column 1 - "Event, Situation, or Person (be specific as possible), that Triggered Me Anger"

Column 2 - "Anger Scale" Use a scale of 1-10 to indicate how angry you were about this situation/person.

Column 3 - "Body Part Affected". (Which/which parts of your body felt a reaction?)

Column 4 - "Physical Sensations". (How did that particular body area feel like?)

Example:

Column 1 - My boyfriend was late to our date. The more I waited, I felt more frustrated. He was 15 mins late! He understands that I don't like waiting and that I don't like being late!"

Column 2: 8.

Column 3 - Heart, Stomach and Hands, Head, Shoulders and "Brain".

Column 4: The heart beats so loudly and fast that it almost feels like it is actually there.

Stomach - Rumbling, in knots. Also, I was also burping a lot.

Hands/Arms – I alternate between lying on my stomach and rubbing them while moving back and forth.

Shoulders - sore, painful and tensed

Brain - I have trouble remembering much. All I can remember is how angry I am, what I was going on with it and how I would react to his arrival.

Do this exercise as soon as you have experienced an "anger episode." If you need support, your boyfriend can help you by telling you that this is what you feel when he is late. This might be an opportunity to ask your boyfriend for support and reflect on why he is late. Could it be feeling abandoned or disrespected? These are the things you can discuss with your counsellor and/or support group.

Gender Socialization as Anger and Gender Expression of Anger

It is impossible to laugh and be angry at the same time. Anger or laughter are mutually exclusive. However, you can choose to be angry or happy.

Wayne Dyer

"Never, ever argue at night. It is the worst thing you can do to your sleep.

"You can't settle any issue until morning anyway."

Rose Kennedy

Anger is a subjective emotion that everyone experiences differently. A person's anger might not have any effect on another person. Men and women see, express and manage anger differently.

"Men seem able to accept their anger and use them to their advantage, while women perceive anger as being counterproductive." It seems that women don't feel comfortable with feeling angry. They also don't like expressing their anger. Women tend not to express their anger.

Researchers attribute these differences in behavior to the fact assertiveness and self-promoting behaviors are seen as masculine traits. Men can express their anger inwardly. Women, however, are considered unfeminine.

Another interesting observation was men expressing ineffectiveness if their anger is not released outwardly. Women, however, do not seem to share this feeling. Contrary to what you might think, women generally feel that anger can cause them distress and make it difficult for them. To cope with this, they hide, control and sometimes even apologize.

These "gender structures" partially influence and impact both genders' anger expression.

It seems that for women in particular, feeling justified to feel angry and being able to show their anger requires some assertiveness as well as confidence.

In the following sections, we will talk more about assertiveness as a method of managing anger.

Anger Management: Expressing Not Suppressing versus Anger Solutions

"The opposite side of anger is calmness, it's empathy."

Mehmet Oz

Anger can be a "normal" emotion that everybody experiences. It is a normal response when faced with a danger situation. It is your body's way protecting you.

Certain parts of your brain, such as your limbic system and emotional brain, activated when there is a great threat to your ability to react immediately. Your body reacts by making you more alert, your eyes widen and your heart rate faster to pump blood to your system. Also, your breathing speed increases which aids in the oxygen delivery to your cells.

You also have your "thinking mind", which is the part that influences your emotions.

This is the part that allows for you to think and act more rationally. It also helps you be more responsible in future situations.

Uncontrolled or unmonitored aggression can cause unwanted side effects. It can affect your relationships and work performance as well as cause problems with authorities. Even though anger may not lead to violence, aggression, or hostility in all cases, these are possible consequences if it is not controlled.

Recognize signs that your anger is growing out of control. Seek out help. Do not feel weak by seeking help. To the contrary, seeking out help is a sign you are strong, have a strong sense to responsibility and are willing to do whatever it takes to make things better for yourself and others.

There are many resources that you could explore. You can begin your search online. You can find many support groups for mood disorders online, as well as those for anger management. There are also groups that are exclusively for women. You can be as specific as your age, marital status and religion. the best one for you.

Face-to-face support groups for anger management are the best, provided that you are available and willing to participate. Your participation and willingness to attend the group sessions on a regular basis, as well as your diligence in performing the suggested exercises, will greatly impact your success rate.

Be patient with you. It will take some time. It might be difficult at first. You might be tempted just to quit. You will see improvements as you keep at it.

There are many places that offer anger management classes. Also, there are counselors and psychiatrists as well as social workers and psychiatrists. This can be quite expensive.

Your decision is up to each of you. One of the benefits of joining a group is that it allows you to share, learn and exchange experiences with other members. You are able to build a community with your peers.

Canada's Mental Health Association, (CAMH), developed the "Anger Solutions" Program. It was founded on anger management concepts. There are some differences between the two. First and foremost is the terminology used to describe the program's philosophy.

According to CAMH, anger management is teaching people how CONTROL something. Anger Solutions is all about overcoming anger and the Issues that can bring it up. We address the root causes of people's anger and help them to find new ways to respond. It is not necessary to teach them how control their behaviour, because they have learned something more valuable: how to handle their emotions safely and appropriately. "The behavioural change is a result of this (and some coaching from facilitators).

The other distinction between anger management and the CAMH's Anger Solutions Program is that Anger Solutions is about integrating several therapeutic models that best suit the needs of the client (as opposed to anger management, which utilizes a single model, usually, cognitive-behavioral).

Anger Solutions Program includes the cognitive-behavior approach along with other treatment options such as Reality Therapy and Solution Focused Therapy. It also offers life skills training using the psychosocial rehabilitation model.

Anger Solutions Program's developers believed that if your only tool is a drill, you can treat everything like a nail. Anger Solutions provides a complete toolkit and not just a hammer.

CAMH reports that this approach has been very successful ever since it was first developed. This is because it keeps clients motivated, which in turn reduces attrition or dropout rates. This increases the chances of a client successfully completing their program.

Last but not the least, forgiveness is a crucial component of the Anger Solutions Approach. The creators believe it is a powerful tool that can help people release any hurts they have experienced and is essential to the healing process.

Women, especially those from strong religious backgrounds, have a lot of guilt or shame.

Many times, women don't fully understand the reasons they feel ashamed of. This can lead them to harbor anger and hostility toward themselves and others. These cases can lead to anger and hostility. It is possible to forgive yourself and others.

Chapter 12: Learning To Walk (Again), Low-Risk Interactions

Your comfort zone is about be taken over by someone else. It's because you're going out of it. Learning to walk again will help you overcome your fear and rejection.

Avoid sweating. It's not going to be easy, but it's going change everything. You're tired to feel trapped. You're ready and able to stop worrying. So, relax. You can do it.

The rest of this book includes practical exercises to help you see the world less threatening and give you room to grow.

Exercise 1

You're always entering a new world every time you leave your home. However, a lot of these opportunities are dependent on your engagement in the world around.

You will have to stop hiding behind your earbuds, a kindle or other mobile device if you want to get out of the habit of doing that. For those who fear rejection, technology is often used as a way to isolate themselves. It acts as a buffer to keep you from a world that is threatening. The seeds of rejection are all around.

Your next outing will be without you except for your welcoming smile. No tech buffers.

I won't assume you use public transportation to go to work or do chores. But I will hope you do. Because public transit has many opportunities to engage in casual activities.

It's easy to boost your confidence with small acts such as offering a seat to an elderly rider and allowing someone to take the train or bus ahead of you. Since no one is against courtesy, this is a low risk activity.

If you're too nervous to speak up, you don't need to open the mouth. You can just smile and get up from the seat, tilting your heads and signaling with your hand that it's yours. You can either step aside or allow another rider to board in front of you.

It's easy. It's easy. You are also acknowledging the existence and needs of others.

If you don't use public transportation, You're going be courteous and allow other drivers merging. You won't let another driver park in your spot. You will be a shining example of driving virtue.

You take no chance. You're setting an example to others and you're making a positive impression on yourself.

While these low-risk behavior may not seem essential, they can help get you out of your suffocating cocoon and into the light of a better day.

Chapter 13: Tests For Determining Your Type Of Perception

Let's now look at more accurate methods to determine your type, namely psychological tests. Here are three tests to consider. The following tests are suggested. You don't have to do them in the same order. This will enable you to obtain more reliable results as well as aid you in self-knowledge. However, the most important part is that the testing will not only help you to determine which type of perception is the strongest and weakest, but also identify which one you are most comfortable with. This valuable information is what you will need to continue your work in intelligence development to properly wire your mind.

Test 1

You can decide whether or not to agree with each statement. If you agree with each statement, you can place a (+) sign next the appropriate approval number. If you disagree, you can put a (-) (minus) sign. It is imperative to respond quickly and clearly without hesitation.

For me to be able concentrate on work that requires silence I must have it.

Results

If there are eight of more pros, you're kinesthetic.

Compare the numbers of pulses within each of the three groups. Your active way of perceiving is the one that has them most clearly. The one where there are less than eight is your second-degree perception. The one with less than eight represents your weak link - the type of perception that is least developed.

You may get the same number benefits from each of the three options. This means that there is not just one type of perception. Both are basic and develop approximately equally.

If you have roughly the same number advantages in all three groups, then every type of perception is developed evenly. True, it is rare. This happens mainly in people who have previously engaged in the development their visual, hearing, and kinesthetic capabilities.

Test 2

Put a score between 1 and 5 in each of the three statements. 1 - It doesn't concern me, 2 - It happens very rarely but sometimes", 3 – "Sometimes it happens", 4, & 5 – "Pretty often",

Group 1

Results

Count how many points you have in each group. If you have a maximum result of 1 in each group, then it is visual. Group 2 and 3 are audial and kinesthetic. Next, find out which type or perception is weaker.

3. Test

Without wasting your time, pick the closest answer to each question from the list.

1. You need to try something new, whether it's to build furniture, sew, or plant a tree. How would you prefer to behave?

A. This is how it works.

B. Ask for advice from knowledgeable people.

C. It is possible to figure it yourself.

2. You came to our library to pick up a book to take on vacation. What book would you pick?

A. With illustrations, travel notes

B. Psychological detective, or melodrama.

C. The book about nutrition and healthy living.

3. Writing a letter, article or report and not knowing the correct spelling of a word, can lead to confusion. There is no dictionary. How will your behavior be?

A. A.

B. B.

C. Choose the option you intuitively feel is the best.

4. You visited a brand new company. What is the first thing you think of when you are done?

A. A.

B. Names of people but not faces or clothing.

C. The overall environment and how you felt.

5. There will be an exam. How do you prepare for the exam?

A. Take the time to read the book and take notes.

B. Retell the material that you have just learned aloud.

C. Write quick cheat sheets on cards to be hung on walls and studied while on the move.

6. Imagine that you have in front a large, white piece of paper where "apple" has been written large. What's your initial reaction to this situation?

A. A.

B. B.

C. The apple smell and taste was familiar to you.

7. It is important to be able to focus, concentrate, use your mental abilities, and complete difficult tasks. What could be the biggest obstacle?

A. A.

B. B.

C. Poor posture, tight clothes, or shoes

8. You find yourself in a situation where you are forced to wait - such as waiting in line for an appointment. How should you behave?

A. Pay attention to your surroundings and pay close attention to people.

B. B.

C. Hold something in your hand, walk back and forth or trampel it.

9. The exhibition attracted you. What inspection method would you prefer more?

A. A.

B. Use the audio guide to join the tour.

C. To walk without a plan from picture to photograph - "where your legs will take me."

10. Somebody behaved in a way that you consider unworthy. What should you do?

A. A.

B. This is what you should think.

C. Show your willingness to leave or maybe you knock your fists on the table, or you slam it loudly.

11. You received very good news. How should you respond?

A. Smile, your eyes are sure to shine with joy.

B. A monologue about how excited you are.

C. Jump up and clap you hands.

12. You've heard a song that you liked. What are YOU doing?

A. It is possible to visualize what is being sung.

B. Sing along.

C. Step into the rhythm of your foot or dance to it.

13. A fascinating story happened to you. You want others to hear it. How can you make it the best?

A. Would write about it.

B. Orally.

C. Played with the faces.

14. Imagine that you were invited for dinner at a restaurant. Even though you were fully satisfied with the food, you still didn't like the place. Why?

A. The interior was unappetizing.

B. The singer had a bad voice.

C. It was stuffy and hot or cold or uncomfortable chairs or tables.

Processing the results

Calculate how many answers are A, B, C and how many B. If A dominates, you are visual. B is audial. C is kinesthetic. The number of answers will determine which type you have in second, and which in third.

Chapter 14: Prayer: The Ultimate Solution To Frustration In Life

A day spent feeling angry, frustrated or depressed is still a worthwhile day. This is the first time I've shared this story with you. It's been a difficult day for me. I was depressed and angry. This has been one the most challenging days of my life in months. I will be sharing with you my strategies for getting through these days, and how I still believe they're worthwhile.

Life is fine even when it's hard. Things will eventually get better. This makes a difference. I used to be frustrated and downhearted, thinking that life would never get better. I believed things would remain the same because it is what they are. There is no way for things to get better if I do something different or change something. Today I know that things will get better if they don't get worse.

My wife and i have been discussing various things today. I'm having a lot of trouble and that has not always meant I didn't make things worse. Most days I am able to recall what I shared with you. That has helped me to have much better days.

My wife and my life has been more challenging than this. The reason they were so difficult was because I kept making things worse. I am able to stop having angry thoughts and realize that they are not necessary. Those thoughts aren't connected to what I actually do.

If I find myself thinking of things that could be considered violent, angry or nefarious, those thoughts can actually help. Those thoughts show me how unhappy and hurtful I am. They motivate me and help me pray.

It would be much more difficult for me to learn and get help if my thoughts were only about flowers and walking in the clouds. Sometimes the most rewarding learning comes from pain and frustration. It's a wonderful time to be in pain, suffering, or frustration and ask for help.

Today is a great moment and I'm happy to share this with you. And, believe me, I tried hard to avoid writing this section today. However, if you avoid doing what you're doing and having a hard time, how are I going to be able share the value that it has for you?

Two results can be obtained from the same topic of difficulty. You will get the result of your problems. Everyone will then make you feel as though you aren't good enough. When you're having a difficult time starting with, the last thing that you want is for someone to come in and help you.

Today, I am much more comfortable talking about what I do and accepting that sometimes that result might not be my best.

Another fear I have is that people might not be willing to help me. People will not listen to me if it is something I struggle with.

Today I share because the overall result is worth every bit of trouble. I keep moving forward because I know it won't get worse and I will work to make it better.

I'm currently playing League of Legends. I try to do the exact same things on both a good and bad day. A bad day used to cause me anxiety. I used to listen to certain songs when I was feeling down. I would either try to use alcohol to soothe the pain or take up too much exercise and work.

Today, no matter what the day brings me, I try to do the same thing. Because I know things work out well on a positive day, it gives me peace and security that they will get better. When things are working well, then they can turn a bad day into a good one.

In other words, it helps to keep it from getting worse. I often tried new things during bad days. I would make such big promises, and switch things up. I would schedule my days if I was having bad days. I would schedule my new routine and diet. I often made bad choices. They were compensated choices, made more out of a bad than a good feeling. Instead of finding a healthy diet, I will punish myself by trying this diet.

If you're feeling good, bad days can seem very foreign. If everything is going great, why would you do that? Why would anyone want to eat that diet? I'm capable of handling it, and can eat as much or little as I like. I can't eat anything I don't like on bad days, so I need to stay true to my diet.

Talking about the things you are experiencing is a great way to gain perspective. It's incredible to see that people around me can have difficult days, even if I think I'm having one. It's amazing how you can find others who are going through a difficult day. In fact, almost everyone in your family and circle of friends will have a bad day.

It's not helpful to me to make negative comments about other people or say that I'm having bad days because of it. My reactions to life are the root of my bad days. My wife has not done anything to cause me to have a bad week. It's not her actions, it's how I react to them. My lack love and understanding is what has made me feel hurt. When I love and understand others, everyone is free to do whatever they want.

If I love and get to know you, you are free to do what you wish. I don't care if you steal, copy, or do something bad about me. I've heard a lot of negative things online about me.

I feel better when I'm in a loving relationship. I do not recall ever saying anything bad. I know that when I was in a difficult situation and had to say bad things, it was necessary for me to get help. It is easy to overlook a day such as today and not notice it when it is hard.

I had so much success in the last year that it gave me this false sense that there is no other day like it. Some days, I am able to remember that it's all worthwhile. There is nowhere better than where I live and this is what I should be doing. This is what I want and where I should go. A good day at The Core and the Foundation is just another day alive. It's not the same as a day you might call bad, full of despair, anxiety, hurt, and hate.

It's easier to see all of the life in this way. It's possible to see how your bad and good days are all part of the wonderful life you live.

This is an honor and a privilege to share with you. It's easy to talk about my hobby, but it's a different thing to do it. This League of Legends Game is the perfect way to practice what you have shared with me and to play it as normal. It doesn't matter how much of a day I have, this game will still be enjoyable.

We had a little bit more trouble up top while I tried hard to help the guy. It was difficult but rewarding to be able keep my cool. We had a lot of fun playing the game. I survived the first disaster and didn't lose my cool. Keep your attitude positive and you will be able to overcome any challenge.

I'm thankful to have discovered that even when it was difficult, every detail was another reason to turn around. I'm thankful that I don't currently have any reason to flip out. I've made a lot silly mistakes in the game like purchasing an item that was not right, and I have a great wit about it. I always try to do my best, and everyone on my team does their best. That's all that matters.

Even though I played badly and even though my mom called throughout, I am grateful that we won. It doesn't matter if we win. Good things can happen even when it's not the best day. They might not be perfect but they are enough. I'm thankful for that today.

Today, I pray to remember my gratitude for living in spite of all the emotions. I ask today that I don't make it worse regardless of what happens. I also pray for you today.

If you are going through a divorce, there are two options. Either stay in your pain or get over it.

I believe that you would choose to do the latter. To move on in your life.

Forgiving yourself for your mistakes and allowing yourself to forgive is part of moving forward in life.

It's not always easy. However, finding true love again doesn't have to seem so scary. To make this happen, all you need is a plan. You will continue wandering the streets in the hope that you find true love, no matter how hard it may seem.

These are the seven steps that you should take now to make love again.

For those who have suffered a painful breakup, here is a 7-step fail-proof plan to find real love after a difficult one

STEP ONE: Let Go Of Your Ex

If you aren't ready to let go of your ex then it will be hard to find true love.

Your mind is unable to let go of your ex without consciously thinking about it.

Do you feel bad about your breakup today? Do you feel stuck in anger, blame and bitterness? It's time to let go.

Your ex will most likely have moved on. Most likely, they are living their best lives. Do you think this is what you are still holding onto? What are you doing to yourself?

STEP TWO. Believe you have more than one soulmate

It is funny how some people feel after a breakup that it has ended their chance at being with their soul mate for a lifetime.

Think of it this way: your soulmate is the person you get to spend your entire life with. Not the one you broke it up with.

It can be very hard to feel the pain of breaking up. But, you shouldn't lose the chance of your dreams.

The one person that will never leave your life is the one I know. This is the one person who brings out all of your best and who loves you with all their heart. They are the one who makes you feel loved, special, adored, and cherished. And don't ever let a relationship go bad or make it difficult for yourself to find the one.

Find new, incredible people and go out. Stop limiting yourself to having one soul mate. Do not let yourself be deprived of the love and support that is available to you.

STEP THREE

Some people vow to never be friends with their ex after a split. People believe that the only way to make it work is to find someone who is totally different from their ex.

This is, at best, a knee-jerk reflex from hurt, and not one well-informed by your senses.

Instead of trying to find someone who is the exact opposite of your ex, it's better to be focused on the right things.

What are these right items? Now you have a question? Read step four.

STEP 4: Be Clear About Your Values

If you are looking for love, the biggest mistake people can make is to get involved with someone that doesn't share your values.

However, to attract the person who shares your values, you need to be clear about what they are.

It helps you to direct your life by having a set value system. It helps you understand what to accept, and what to reject. It will teach you how to behave. Who to date and whom not to.

Most relationships fail because of people who have different values and come together to fool themselves. Their love-tinted glass eventually falls apart and they discover that they never shared anything. It is then painful for them to look at their individual paths.

Do not give in to this temptation. Be true to your values. Seek out the one person with similar values to yours.

STEP FIVE. Avoid Relationships That Waste Your Time

As humans, we don't like letting people down. We don't like making others feel rejected and hurting them. This is why it's difficult to say "no"

In order to have a healthy relationship, you need to be able and willing to turn down proposals from others. It's more about how you feel and what you think.

You will waste both your time as well as theirs if you wait to say "no" when you know that a relationship won't work out. As you have both put off saying no, it will become more difficult to say yes.

You must be respectful when you tell the other person that things are not going to work out. You should speak from a place that is honest and shows compassion. Make sure you are clear and concise in what you say.

In the short term, they may feel hurt or rejected by your actions. In the end, however, they will respect you more for being truthful with them, even if they feel hurt or rejected.

STEP SIX. Find ways to improve your self

If you are going through a divorce, take some time to reflect on the things that could have been done differently.

Don't blame yourself for this. Don't be too hard on yourself. Everyone can improve in some areas of their lives. You are no different. Do this while focusing on being the best version possible of yourself.

Do not hesitate to read books and attend trainings. Do whatever you can do to improve your weaknesses and increase your strength.

It's easy to blame the other person when they do wrong. However, this will never help you to grow. Instead of dwelling upon what your ex did wrong, instead focus on how you can grow. Here is the place where you can grow and improve.

STEP SEVEEN: Do It!

You can't find love in a closed room. If you really want to find your new love, then you need to get out and do it.

Some people have the fantasy that the universe will somehow send them love one day. Well, get over it. It doesn't work that way. It's up to you if it must!

It's amazing what happens when you are willing to step out of your comfort zone and confront your fears.

Don't worry if this is your first time. Get involved in the community by finding common interests. Talk to someone new on the bus. You might also consider trying online dating.

You don't have to obsess about finding new love. You'll have to let the process unfold at its own pace. There is no pressure. Give yourself enough time to feel love again.

Chapter 15: Rejection In Relationships

Rejection in relationships, especially romantic ones can be painful and embarrassing. In most societies, men approach women first for relationships. This is often because the men don't feel comfortable approaching women and fear rejection. It can be demoralizing for a man to get rejected by a woman (rejection) and it can also lead to anxiety about approaching women.

This can happen to women as well. A woman may be attracted to him (crush), and she might even give him green light (show indirect interest) hoping that he will ask her out. Then suddenly, another woman asks out. This will result in her being disappointed and sad (rejection).

Rejection can also occur between friends, in peer groups. This is where a group can bully or ignore one another, thereby making that person feel isolated. It doesn't matter how we view it, rejection is painful and can lead to depression.

Chapter 16: Rejection In Marriage

This is another kind of rejection that can make one feel hurt. This is because it comes from one's partner. He or she is supposed to be your lover or husband or wife.

Most often, in marriage, men are the ones initiating sex. If their spouse says no, it can hurt their spirits and bruise their ego. It makes them feel rejected, and can lead to a lack of self confidence. This can also be vice-versa.

The women feel the most rejected when their husbands refuse to eat the food they prepare. Although most women believe that the only way to a man's heart lies through his stomach, it can be disappointing when a man refuses to eat food that a woman prepared.

If one of the spouses rejects the suggestions or opinions of the other, it can be a rejection in marriage. A man might suggest a type of building/house that isn't suitable for the woman and she may reject it.

It is possible to feel rejected if one of the partners violates their marital vows. Cheating can range from withholding affection or withholding love, to having a physical or sexual affair with another. This can cause depression in one partner, and it can make them doubt their ability or willingness to have a sexual relationship with another partner.

Sometimes, in certain African cultures, women are treated more favorably than their male counterparts. This can lead to rejection of marriage. When a married woman gives birth to only boys, both her husband or her in-laws will reject her and throw her out of her matrimonial residence. Because they are married to another man, these girls are not eligible for inheritance.

These are the main reasons that couples get divorced in a marital relationship.

Chapter 17: Rejection At Work/Family

Not only can rejection happen in a relationship, but it can also happen at work or in the family. This cannot overemphasized.

I will take myself as an example. After I finished college, I was looking forward to a series job interviews and the possibility of getting hired. After many failed attempts, I was finally able to pass a bank interview. At that moment, I felt elated by the idea of becoming a banker. On the day I was supposed get my appointment letter, I got a letter telling me that I was not chosen for the job. I was devastated by this rejection and felt a lot of sadness and hopelessness. The feeling of being useless began to creep in. This is one example of many times we feel rejected.

Some people believe they are hoping to be promoted because they have put so much work into an office. But, their colleague got the promotion, and they were left behind. Some people give credit to their coworker for their contribution to a project. Others get fired.

People in marketing departments know that it is being rejected from potential clients. They have gone to market hoping to find a patron, only to receive a "No" (rejected).

Although rejection from spouses and peer groups can be devastating, it is also very painful to receive it. However, family rejection can impact other areas of life and cause havoc when left untreated. Sometimes one child is more intelligent than another. A couple might give birth to an autistic baby. Rejected children will become timid and vulnerable to bullying. They will withdraw and find it difficult to defend themselves. Others will see and treat them badly.

Another habit of some parents is to praise their kids who are rich and extol them while treating their not so rich children with disdain.

These are just a few of the many ways family members may reject you. However, it is clear that rejection from family members can lead to feelings of inadequacy, low self-esteem, and a negative effect on your future relationships.

However, no matter what the rejection may be, one thing remains constant, pain. And we must find a way of healing, dealing with it, and setting ourselves free.

I have 12 guides to help you overcome any shame, pain or breakup.

Chapter 18: Practical Guides On How You Can Overcome Rejection

Rejection is a natural part of being human. It is impossible to succeed in love and life without experiencing rejection. We all experience it. However, those times that we do face rejection are often the ones we feel most isolated and castaway.

A lot of the pain and hurt experienced when we feel rejected is not caused by the actual loss. Instead, it is the stories we tell ourselves about the experience. Studies show that our response to rejection is largely determined by what we have done in the past, such our attachment history. The way we respond to rejection is often just as amazing or even better than the rejection itself. These are the reasons we have a lot more power to build our response to rejection.

There are many different methods you can use to deal with rejection. These tools and methods can include psychological tools, such as reflecting on our past and improving our self-understanding.

Here are some highlights from our most powerful personal game plan to help you deal with rejection. These are their key points:

Shift your outlook/view

The way we view rejection can influence how we respond to it. Research shows that how a person views their personality and recovers from or stays stuck in rejection can have a significant impact on how they handle it. People who view their personalities as more solid and are less likely to blame other people for the breakup will have a more stable mentality. Rejection can cause them to look down on themselves and make a lot of excuses. They may also be less optimistic about the future. People with a developmental mindset see their personalities as something they can alter or evolve. They see the breaking up as an opportunity to change and grow. They believe their romantic future will improve and that their relationships will improve. People who have a developmental mindset are more likely to heal emotionally after a breakup. When we embrace the idea that life doesn't have to be complicated and that every loss is an opportunity for us to learn, we are able to experience greater growth and less suffering from rejection.

Embrace Your Uniqueness/Individuality

If we listen to the analytical side of our brains, it's easy to feel more insecure and less confident after a rejection. You may feel some sort of pain after you end a relationship. It might be painful or difficult for some people or places to be reconnected with. However, this moment is an opportunity for us to truly connect with our individuality. Whatever makes us shine, whatever it may be, we should try to find it. Try new things to discover the new opportunities that are available. Discovering new things can help us discover more about ourselves. Remaining connected to people that matter and are vital to us shows that we can have a full life, regardless of the rejections we suffered. And that life will continue.

Take a deep breath and learn some personal care.

The immediate aftermath of a rejection is hard to process because we are so overwhelmed by pain. You will likely feel anger and hurt immediately after a rejection. But, contrary to popular belief/opinions, releasing anger (for example, hitting a punching ball or shouting at someone) doesn't help reduce that negative emotion. It is more likely to increase it.

These moments are when personal care is crucial. Activities like running, going for a walk, meditation, or yoga can all help to balance your mind and make it easier to focus on the facts and not get lost in emotion. You can also try other activities that make you feel happy and help you relax, such as reading, baking, or listening to music.

Pay Attention To Your Inner Detractor

We are affected by everything that happens to us as human beings. But we also have an impact on the screen we use to view it. Research has shown that the inner voice of the analyst can have a significant impact on how people see the world. This inner critic works in our heads to attack, undermine and derail us, much like a cruel coach. The same way that we build a healthy sense and self-esteem through positive and nurturing experiences, our inner critic can also be formed by negative experiences early in life that give us the fundamental feeling that we are wrong or bad. It's a kind of "anti-self," a side of us that is turned against ourselves, and it can be found throughout our lives.

The voice symbolises a destructive thought that often harms us in life as well as in relationships. Sometimes, it attacks us when we are least vulnerable. If we feel rejected, the voice will remind us to "See? I warned you, you'd fail. There is no one who could possibly like you. You will never find the thing you want. You will always be rejected" This also leads to bad advice: "You shouldn't ever have put yourself out here. It is impossible to trust anyone again. You will only get hurt. "No need to try again"

We are all flawed and human. Most likely, we have things that we want to improve on. But this voice doesn't make us feel welcome and is not conducive towards real change. It perpetuates self destructive thinking, which can sometimes lead to selflimiting or self destructive actions. If we can be on our own side, or with our closest friend, it is much easier to cope with a breakup and move on. You should make your analytical inner voice your number one enemy when dealing with a breakup. Experts suggest that we identify these voices and separate them from our analytical inner voice.

It is important to take this seriously when we go through a breakup.

Rosy Pictures Don't Look Back

Rejection often leads to a greater tendency to build up those who are rejecting us. Sometimes, rejection can make jobs seem more appealing. If they don't return calls, it can make dates seem more attractive or attractive. Even relationships that were painful or miserable can suddenly seem happy. When we're grieving for something we don't remember, it can be more difficult to accept rejection.

People who struggle with intimacy or closeness often have a certain degree of what's called "fantasy-bond," an illusion of security and connection that replaces genuine love, intimacy, and affection. They accept being in a relationship just for the sake. However, they lose out on the true respect, warmth, or attraction that brought them together. The relationship ends when one of them decides to end it. However, the other person mourns the relationship. They tend to forget about or ignore the struggles and fights they had, the parts that didn't mesh with the other person and the characteristics they disapproved of in the relationship. If we feel rejected, even though we feel angry at the situation, we often find ourselves more willing to take the other person apart while strengthening the one who rejects us. We love the person or the relationship and feel compelled to keep it. But, at the same time, we reinforce the belief that our worth is less or unworthy. This feeling of unworthiness can often be rooted in deep inside of us. The reality of what we have lost is less important than the core negative feeling about our self that drives us to believe that fantasy is better than reality.

Do not hide from your pain.

It is easy to judge yourself and it is wasteful. However, if we are going through a painful time in our lives, it is best not to try to suppress or ignore our feelings. Allow yourself to feel the sadness, anger, or frustration that comes up when you feel rejected. Some feelings are more severe than others. They can also trigger older, more important emotions. This can lead to us feeling more afraid of these feelings and leading us to attack ourselves or the person who has rejected. You can choose how you behave. Although we shouldn't let our feelings dictate how we behave in any way, it doesn't mean we have to stop them from being expressed. It may be better to allow ourselves to feel our emotions, but remember that emotions come in waves. To deal with emotional overwhelm or pain, it's best to seek help. Sometimes we feel relieved when our sadness is allowed to be felt. It is possible to feel lighter and more in control of the circumstances.

Do self-empathy

Research has shown that divorced couples who were self-empathetic reported having fewer negative thoughts about their divorce and less bad dreams. They also had less negative contemplation. Self-empathy ranks high among all variables that predict how people will feel after a divorce.

These three essential elements can be described as self-empathy.

Self-kindness is better than self-assessment. If we feel our analytical inner voice infiltrating and clouding our outlook, then we should strive to be self-kind. In other words, we need to treat ourselves like a friend would. Our own struggles are important and we need to be understanding and compassionate. This does not mean feeling sorry for oneself, not feeling weak, not denying our mistakes and not being judgmental.

Common humanity versus isolation: Studies have shown there is no single way to overcome the feeling of being trapped. Each human being has suffered, and many have been rejected. It is possible to keep this connection in our minds and avoid feeling disconnected or different. Many people have experienced a similar journey, so it is important to be optimistic and connected in the future.

Over-identification or consciousness? Consciousness and awareness are two different things. Consciousness allows us to be fully present in the moment, and we learn to meditate freely without judgment. Aside from having many benefits for mental and physical wellbeing, consciousness can also help us avoid over-identifying with any negative thoughts or feelings. Without allowing negativity to overtake, we can feel our emotions. We can avoid becoming a slave to the "analytical inner thoughts" that distort reality and exaggerate our feelings. It is possible to calmly feel calmer through mindful meditation and breathing exercises when emotions or reactions are strong.

Self-empathy helps us be kind to ourselves, even when we feel rejected. While being truthful to ourselves, and the circumstances, we can still be kind and understanding.

Avoid using victimization or being used

Recognizing and feeling our feelings is vital. But it's not helpful to dwell on or be victimized by the circumstances. It is easy to become angry after a rejection and to obsess about our circumstances. This can lead you to feel victimized or used. We get stuck in our suffering, not feeling like we have any power. Our attitude can either be sluggish, demoralized, and charged with anger or sluggish from victimized feelings. It is crucial to be honest in all aspects of your actions, even when you feel the most hurt and vulnerable. Although self-empathy is something we should continue to practice, it's important to recognize that this does not mean feeling or acting like a victim.

Allow your emotions to be processed.

After taking time to calm down, get grounded and take some time to think clearly about what you are thinking or feeling. You can do this by getting a pen to paper and writing it down in black & white. It is possible to take a list of all the emotions that you feel, and then write down the thoughts that go with them. Doing this will allow you to create distance. You'll be able better handle rejection because you won't get entangled in it.

Paying attention to your emotions is important. It's not helpful to feel pressured to feel something. Your emotions do not have to be right or wrong. Give yourself permission to feel whatever you like.

Practice Self-assertiveness

Instead of just acknowledging your emotions you can write some positive things about your self. In other words, make a list of your strengths, values, and worth. Then, start each morning by reading them aloud to yourself. It's not enough to talk about yourself. You need to think about who you are. Self-assertiveness can be used to help you hold on to the things that make you unique. This will allow you to become stronger in spite of rejection.

Spend time with your loved ones. Or just think about them.

You will be rejected by anyone, so it is important that you remember that there is more to life that the rejection from one person or thing. There are many others who can help you. Keep in touch with people you care about and spend quality time with them to remind you that you aren't completely rejected or ignored by the world. To help you deal with rejection by a crush, it might be a good idea to reach out to your friends and get some moral support.

Connection is so important because we remember all the things that are not in our memory at the moment. It reminds we of how beloved we are...that people care...that we are valuable and that they love us.

Even if your relationship with your loved one is not possible right now you can take the time to connect with them. Even better, find a picture of them. Ideally, it should be a photo of the two of you having fun. Keep this photo in your mind and remind you that you are supported and cared for by this person each day.

It is possible to repeat this and look at the pictures and you will start to hold it in your heart stronger. You can then refer to that image, even if it is just meditation, when you feel overwhelmed or rejected.

Connect to your Past

Understanding how we respond to rejection can be helped by looking back on our past events. It is common for painful past events to trigger emotions in the present. One example is that we may be more open to suffering from a loss if we experienced an insecure attachment early in life. Unconsciously, as adults, we seek to revive the emotional environment of our past even though it was painful. People who are more accepting or less open to us may be the ones we choose. We may be more attracted to those or circumstances that make it seem like we feel the same way about ourselves. This personal report is from someone who was rejected. It shows how being able to connect with your past and having a clear understanding of it can help you deal with rejection.

THE POWERFUL ATTRACTION AND REJECTION

All I want is for him. He is the only one I will ever fall in love with, and the only one with whom I will ever feel that way. What happened? Why did he stop being my lover? Don't stop longing after me. How can I make him love me again? If only I could find the answer. Will he really love me if i get in shape, dress as he likes and help him with his chores? I don't understand it. What is it? He loved me, and he wanted me. This is making my wild. I must figure it all out. It has to be fixed. He needs to give me his love and attention.

Only I can. He is finished. He has moved on, his passion, his desire to please me, have all disappeared. He lost it. I don't know the reason. He stopped yearning to be with me over the years. He began to drive away and avoid me when it was me who wanted him. Many nights I lay awake, dreaming and lonely, wanting. His body was next to mine but all the warmth, all the desire, it was gone!

Is it possible to have someone who isn't done with me, but why? What are you yearning to get? Why am I so desperate to find my love back? How can I permit a man who has abandoned me to have my thoughts and so much of mine? It is obvious that something is wrong. It is excessive; he is far too much. It is not in proportion. He doesn't deserve this level. Why? Why are you doing this? And then, I get it. I know he doesn't want to me but more importantly, I realize that he is changing. That is what is so compelling.

How can this be fixed? How I got the love back was when I went home. I am seven years old. I live in a house with my mother, who is a reject, and my father, who can only express his feelings for her when she is not there. I am confused. I was able to have my father's affection and attention. But then it disappeared. He doesn't have anything for me. He was only concerned in her safety. I might have suspected that it was not me. Perhaps they were too busy protecting their own children and were unable to provide me with love, consistency, trustworthiness, and genuine love. Instead, I felt rejection, loneliness, which made me realize that something was wrong. I was far too much for her. With him, I wasn't enough. There was nothing that I could have done to make it okay. The love had ended, and the place it left was desperation and loneliness.

This is the problem I want to solve. It isn't about the man I live with today. That is what I can do. I was unhappy. I was not getting what my heart desired. I am a desirable woman. I can have more. It was me. The old me. I tried to find love. This is not what a young child should ever do. Now that I look at him, all I can see is his faded face, I do not feel any emotion. My attention broadens. He is just a man that rejected me. The desperation dulls. Now, I think less about him. He is only a person. He is way off the heights that his rejection of him raised him to.

Rejection has no attraction to me. I no longer need his affection. Showing love to myself, knowing my self, how I was hurt and seeing my parents' shortcomings back then instead of accepting them as my own. Do not try to please someone else. I don't have to get over this pain in order to feel better. I am now okay, and I was okay even back then.

Chapter 19: Signs You Grew up with Emotionally Immature Parents

The sincerely juvenile (EI), guardians can be both frustrating and discouraging. It can be hard to keep a loving parent in your heart who doesn't expect honor or extraordinary treatment but still attempts to control and excuse.

EI parents are not interested in having your feelings heard. This is how a relationship with them is depicted. They don't care much about having an open relationship in which two people are able to connect on a deeper level. EI guardians may not be open to sharing such profound emotions, but it is a great bond that can make the members more valuable.

Every once in a while, you may see a temporary yearning for genuine friendship in them. This keeps you connected. The sad truth is that the closer you are to someone, the less likely they will become distant. It's just like being on the dance floor together with someone who is getting away from your efforts to be close. They ask for your consideration, coupled with your attentiveness about being close, create a push-me-pull-me relationship that leaves one feeling unsatisfied. Your parent is important to you, but it's not possible to have a genuine connection.

Your encounters will sound great to you once you get to know them. Once you have a greater understanding of the EI mind you will want to manage your EI guardians (or any sincerely young individual (EIP), in ways that are less intrusive and allow you to build a stronger relationship with them by knowing what you can expect from them.

It's like having genuine juvenile guardians

EI guardians as well as other EIPs display a unique relationship style. The following ten encounters give you a glimpse of what to expect in a relationship.

1. You feel truly desolate when you are around them

EI guardians raise a lot of self-deprecating children. Your parent might have been physically present but you may have felt alone. While it might seem like you have a family that clings to your EI parent but that is completely different from a genuine parent-child relationship. EI guardians are eager to support their kids but can be awkward with the process. EI guardians can be supportive of you if you are feeling debilitated but they don't know how best to help you get in a bad mood. While they may appear abnormal or fake, they may try to ease the suffering of a distressed child.

2. The results of cooperations are disappointing and uneven.

EI guardians can feel uneven because of their narcissism or restricted compassion. You might think they are entrapped in their own self association. When you try to share something important to them, they are likely to talk over and steer the conversation in another direction.

EI guardians often have their offspring learn more about the issues of their elders than the guardians. EI guardians will need your attention if you're worried, but they won't give any support or empathy if you're not feeling well. EI guardians won't sit down and listen to you. They will instead make superficial arrangements, get annoyed with you, or tell you not stress. Their hearts feel shut down, like there's no place inside that they can reach for solace or sympathy.

3. You feel trapped and restricted.

EI guardians want you to prioritize them and let them handle everything. To achieve this, they can pressurize you with disgrace or responsibility until you do what is required. If you do not comply, they may explode into outrage and fault. Control is commonly used for these types of passionate compulsions. However, I believe this word is misleading. These behavior patterns are more like endurance impulses. They will do anything to feel more in control and safe at the time. Unaware of the consequences, however, they can be very dangerous. It is easy to feel caught in their shallow way of talking. EI guardians have a shallow and egocentric approach to relating which can often make it exhausting to chat with them. They choose to talk about topics with which they feel safe, and then the discussion becomes boring and repetitive.

4. They create the foundation, and you serve as an auxiliary.

EI guardians are highly self-referential. It implies that everything is primarily about them. They will expect you to acknowledge second place when it comes to your requirements. They maximize their own benefits to the extent that you feel less appreciated. They are not looking for an identical relationship. They should be treated as the first. If you aren't able to trust your parents, you may feel uneasy. You may feel powerless against stress, anxiety, and wretchedness by thinking about how a parent might look after you. These are sensible reactions to a childhood climate that left you unable to trust a parent with your needs and protect you from those things that could overwhelm you.

5. They will not be open to you or feel genuinely comfortable.

EI guardians tend to be more sensitive inwardly than their more deep feelings, even though they are extremely responsive. They hate being openly exposed, so they often cover themselves behind a protective outside. They also avoid being too gentle with their children, as this could leave them powerless. They emphasize that they should not show adoration to their guardians as it could diminish their power. Because power is all they know.

EI guardians don't hide their weakness. They can still show extreme emotions when they have to battle with someone else, vent about their feelings, or get mad at their children. However, when they're upset, it doesn't look like they're afraid of what they feel. These uncoordinated feelings are just the arrivals of passionate tensions. It is not the same things as being willing to share your passions. Therefore, it is hard to encourage them. They believe that you should feel the pain of their distress but are opposed to genuine soothing. Assuming that you try and encourage them they may force you away. This makes it difficult for them to accept the help and friendship you offer.

6. They transmit enthusiasm through enthusiastic disease

EI people express their emotions nonverbally, rather than discussing them (Hatfield Rapson & Le 2009), pushing themselves beyond their limits and making others uncomfortable (Hatfield Rapson & Le 2009). This lack of solid limits in family frameworks hypothesis is called enthusiastic combination. It is also called enmeshment in underlying familial treatment. This is how EI relatives can become more integrated into one another's thoughts and feelings.

EI guardians insist that you should intuitively feel what they feel, much like little children. They can feel angry and hurt when you don't meet their needs. They will tell you if you argue with them that they didn't listen enough to what they need. They believe that you should always be sensitive to their needs. It is normal for a child, or little kid, to anticipate such considerations from their parent. However, it is not common for a parent for their youngster to anticipate such considerations from them.

7. They don't respect your boundaries or distinction

EI guardians do not understand the concept of limits. They think that limits are an indicator of dismissal. If they believe this, you won't give them any access to your life. As such, they can be sceptical, hurtful, and insulting if you ask for their security. They don't feel valued if you allow them to stop you. EI guardians search for jobs that are dominant and preferred, where they don't have to be concerned about the limitations of others.

EI guardians won't respect your independence, as they don't see any need for it.

They view family and jobs as sacred and don't see the point in having space or one character separate from them. They fail to understand why you can't just be like them or think like they do, and have similar beliefs and values. You are their child, and in this way you have a place alongside them. In any case, once you're mature, they expect that you will remain their agreeable child or, assuming that you have some control over your life, follow their instructions.

8. You are passionate about the relationship.

Enthusiastic effort is work that you do to accommodate others' needs inwardly. Enthusiastical work can be straightforward such as being a personable and charming, or more complex, such attempting to explain the correct thing to your troubled teen. Passionate work includes sound judgment, empathy, and familiarity with thought processes. It also requires a good deal of intuition about how people will respond to your activities. If things don't go as planned, passionate work becomes essential. For long-term connections, it is important to show passion by saying sorry, seeking compromise, and offering to make things right. EI guardians are interested in fixing relationships and might be unable to help you. EI guardians will often blame others, project fault and claim that they are responsible for their actions. EI guardians can explain that the same thing happened, even though it seems simpler to just say sorry. If you'd known better and done as they requested, this would have never happened.

9. You lose your passion independence and mental opportunities

EI guardians consider you an expansion of their own self, so they ignore your internal universe and thoughts. They reserve the right to judge whether you are being unreasonable or reasonable. They don't value your passion and independence. If you have thoughts that they find offensive, your thoughts will be reflected in their considerations. You are not allowed even to think about particular things in the safety and security of your brain. ("Don't you dare!") The level of their solace is what separates your sentiments from your considerations.

10. They can be downers but, not surprisingly, they can also be savage.

EI guardians may be horrible grouches for their children and other EI beneficiaries. They are not likely to have an effect on the feelings of others, so they won't be able enjoy other people's joy. EI guardians can be supportive and encourage their kids' achievements rather than savoring them. They are known for helping their kids to realize the reality of growing up and disengaging them from fantasies.

Chapter 20: What are Sincerely Juvenile Security Guardians?

If your parent was genuinely juvenile, you might have noticed the following traits in you.

They are determined and unbending, and can become extremely protective when people have other thoughts.

They are low-stress resilient and have trouble allowing themselves to be wronged, limiting current realities and accusing others of not being fair.

They do what feels good, and they often follow the easy way out.

They do not consider the opinions and suppositions that others may have.

They are self-distracted.

They lack empathy and are truly coldhearted.

They did not like sentiments, and could have taught their children that certain sentiments are deplorable or "terrible".

They focus on the physical and not the enthusiastic needs of their young children.

They can be downers by responding in a distrustful or cavalier way to their kids' energy or thoughts.

They can express deep but superficial feelings and are very quick to respond.

As a grown-up you may have the ability to see:

Waiting to feel outrage, dejection and selling out or surrender.

Feeling regretful for being despondent.

Feeling deeply sensitive and discerning towards others.

You may have trouble confiding your impulses.

Fearlessness is not a virtue.

Feeling trapped when dealing with your parents.

Individuals with genuinely juvenile guardians often feel really desolate around their family members, even if they're together. Although there's often a huge emphasis on the essentials that were met by guardians, there is very little attention to the feelings.

This can be challenging for children who have had a parent like this as their parents. They will probably deny their own problems from now on. They could understand that their experience wasn't "Adequately bad" in comparison to the experiences of those who did not have their exact requirements met.

Being a parent means more than giving clothes, shelter, and food to your family. In order for children to be successful adults, they must feel safe and be supported to express their feelings.

Most guardians are too young to pay attention to what they did for their children. Truthfully, we don't have anything to do with these guardians. However, we are trying understand why they behave as they do.

We are here to help you acquire new information about your parent(s), to increase your mindfulness and to give you the opportunity to be more enthusiastic.

Passionate Guardians

The most sincerely young parent is in most cases governed by his or her sentiments. They can respond to little shocks like the apocalypse but will also depend on outside variables such as intoxicants or other substances to balance and relieve them. An emotionally attached parent can swing between being involved in their child's life and abrupt withdrawal. These guardians can be unpredictable and unsteady, and Dr. Lindsay Gibson has called them the most juvenile of all four types of sincerely youthful guardians.

DRIVEN Guardians

A determined parent will generally look the most normal of the four and show the most effort in their children's lives. This is despite the fact that these guardians are extremely controlling and meddling. They seldom stop to show genuine compassion and enthusiasm for their children. All things considered the determined parent is usually occupied and always objectively located. They expect that everyone will have the same needs and be able to esteem them.

Latent Guardians

The latent parent usually abstains from handling any disturbing situations. They are the "#1 parent", often appearing to be more approachable than other types of parents, though only partially. The detached parent is not likely to offer any guidance or cutoff points for their kids in order to aid them in their exploration of the world. They would prefer to be a secondary accomplice to the dominant parent. However, this can lead to misuse and forgetfulness. The latent parent adjusts by limiting issues or assenting.

Guardians should be dismissed

The dismissing guardian must be allowed to be. They rule the family and home often, and everything revolves around their rules. The family intuitively tries not to be irritating. These guardians have little to no relationship or genuine commitment to their children. Their collaborations consist of giving instructions, exploding, and confining themselves from daily life. If the guardian is not allowed to engage in tender or passionate communication with them, they will most likely leave.

Steps to Help Emotionally Immature Parent

Insincere young guardians will make your insane if you fail to recognize their actual age for mental maturation. Recognize the fact that you might have outperformed their formatively at some point in the future, and their inhumanities may start to hurt less.

Is there any moment when you feel like the more mature one in your relationship to your friends? If you assume this, you'll be like many others who feel harmed or baffled every day by their inexperienced guardians. It can be hard to manage guardians without enough compassion to understand the feelings of others. These young guardians focus on their own positives, which can cause their children to feel inferior, inconspicuous and constantly blameworthy.

While the parent who is truly juvenile may seem normal in the outside world, they are able to control their children at home through their own self-involved and controlling behavior. Because they are focused only on their own controlling desires, they can overlook the feelings of their kids. The result is that their kids feel completely alone and out of place.

Just like children, the most youthful guardians are always focused on their needs. They believe that others will expect them to be satisfied first. Their children are unable to fulfill their needs and they subvert their confidence. Their children become rigidly watchful and avoid any passionate kickback if their parent doesn't know what they need.

It is more accurate and valuable to see these guardians as young rather than from the viewpoint of a clinical determination such self-centeredness. They can display a variety of youthful and passionate traits, but not all are diagnosable. It's easier to manage them when they are mentally mature characters than to analyze them.

We instinctively know how to soothe upset babies but we forget to tell our silver-haired guardians. We wouldn't anticipate that a preschooler would be sensitive to our needs, or that they would respond rationally if asked to do something we don't like. Young guardians expect their children to show compassion and sensibility that they do not have. Therefore, we are constantly befuddled and amazed by their responsiveness or resistance. We are left wondering why they try so hard to make everything easy. Were they thinking of us to be different?

Make Use of Your Eyewitness Mentality

Separation from passionate is much more secure than trying to communicate with these guardians. Use your reasoning skills instead of your passionate reaction to avoid being their next victim. In order to be independent from their endorsement, it is important that you observe their self distractions and control moves.

Express, and then Let Go

It's difficult to realize that you won't get a warm response from your parent. It is inexplicably more powerful for you to communicate your thoughts using clear, comfortable correspondence. However, it is also easier to make the assumption that they will change. No matter how emphatic they may answer, it is important to make noise and reinforce your beliefs.

The Relationship is the most important thing.

An honest juvenile parent is unlikely to show empathy or fairness. Consider the end result that you are seeking, not the way the relationship is currently. Anything that is considered private alarms the guardians. Make sure you know what the end result is and then let it all out. While you can request a regret statement, you cannot request a shift or change of perspective.

Make due, Don't Lock in

As opposed to reacting to the parent's statements, engage in discussion. It is important to set clear objectives regarding point and length so that you can guide the discussions towards where they need to be. Your parents will not allow you to be dissatisfied if you don't direct the discussion towards the desired outcome. Assuming they set the pace, you will end up feeling depleted. These guardians will take control of your life and rule over you with their most pressing needs, like their pet meats or neglected necessities. You should not allow their whining or reactions to distract you. Your job is to make things move towards the outcome you desire.

Sincerely juvenile guardians, you will be insane if they fail to realize your actual age for mental growth. It is possible to surpass them in formative skills for a while, but their inhumanities may start to hurt less. You're too young for them to even consider you a possibility.

Chapter 21: How to Deal With Difficult, Anxious, and Disrespectful Siblings

There is no need to be with hazardous people. To add, hazardous family members. So what can we do?

We asked seven specialists to share their best tips on managing irritating, rude and troublesome children.

When you have children who are troublesome, irritating, or discourteous it is difficult to maintain mental health, be calm, and be calm towards them. You may find it difficult to cope with your kin. It is impossible to have an effect on your kin's behavior, but you can influence the way that you respond and answer them. Your kin's behavior is not up to you. You do have control of what their activities mean for you. Next, you will find some ways to ensure that you aren't the subject of family conversation on the next occasion after you had an emotionally explosive and dangerous moment.

Know your bill

You reserve the right not to be the best in the room. You can choose to be treated with respect. You can be mad at someone you love. Understanding your freedoms can help you to put an end to your relationship with your family.

Establish private stopping points with your children

This is the place where you create an imperceptible obstruction on the ground. Tell them how you expect them to behave towards each other. You should let them know what they should do and not share with you, as well as what their consequences will be for violating your boundaries.

You can intellectually set yourself up

Intellectually prepare yourself for family commitments and other occasions where your kin may be. Be aware of how irritating, troublesome and rude your kin may be. But, don't let them get in the way.

Utilize positive self-talk

Remind yourself that you have this. I will not allow them to destroy my day. Be your own mentor. It's similar to a fighter mentally setting themselves up before a fight to prepare.

Rejoice that you don't need to live alongside your kin. It's possible to do anything for a very short time. It is simply about telling yourself that everything will be fine and that you won't allow your kin or family to ruin your day.

It's a daily need to deal with difficult people. It could be at the rec center or at the supermarket. They are annoying and often troublesome. But, how do you deal with irritating people who are your kin

This leaves you with the decision to manage them. The exercise center will not work while you talk to your family if they aren't around at work. These simple mental durability insider facts can make the difference between flipping the top and being able to maintain an even-mind when you are with your troublesome kin.

These are some things that intellectually erratic people do to maintain mental stability

Do not respond, but rather than answering, create opportunities to answer.

When we cooperate with people, we feel one of five different feelings: blissful or miserable, angry, unfortunate, dishonorable, or irate. The automatic response, while answering somebody that has a restricting/rude/irritating perspective, will be accused of feeling.

It is possible to have a "smart and intelligent" reaction when you know that you are in a passionate viewpoint. We can't always monitor our emotions and so we respond to them in ways that are only fueling the flames.

Intellectually intense individuals take the time to listen to what is being said, analyze it with a rational mind, and answer in the same way. They are able to make a difference and create a response.

Be composed even in difficult circumstances

Intellectually driven people can remain cool in difficult situations. They don't allow themselves to be overwhelmed by emotion. They don't allow their emotions to overwhelm them and they keep a sane mind.

They've created a psychological readiness to approach any situation that might arise. As they manage their children, they prepare for any and all that may come before words are spoken. This allows them to mentally prepare themselves for the future by playing out these scenarios.

This gives them the opportunity to plan a reaction, which will ensure they monitor what is going.

Maintain your cool in spite of the unpredictable

Intelligently extreme people are skilled at keeping their head above water in unpredictable situations. They don't allow themselves to be overwhelmed by emotion. They don't allow their feelings to overwhelm them and they keep a clear mind.

They have created a psychological state of readiness that allows them to approach any situation with a smile. As they manage their children, they prepare for any and all that might happen before words are spoken. This allows them to mentally prepare themselves for the future by playing out these scenarios.

This gives them the opportunity to plan a response, which will guarantee that they are aware of what is happening.

Know your triggers

Individuals who are intellectually extreme are extremely aware of their triggers. This is because they have fully simulated scenarios in their brains as to how to respond appropriately to a situation. Because they are extremely aware of their feelings, they are able to draw from similar involvements when experiencing the same thing which makes them happy.

They have created procedures to limit the desire to respond. They have developed procedures to prevent them from acting in a way they fear will upset a relative who presumably did not expect it.

Chapter 22: What is Rejection and How Can It Be Avoided?

Rejection simply means you are rejected. It can also mean you are not valued.

It can be defined as: "to refuse or deny"; "to decide to not use"; "to fail or neglect to provide adequate care or affection." Rejection is a feeling of being rejected. When someone does not want to meet you, they are rejecting you. Rejection is devastating, deadly, debilitating, and destructive. Rejection hurts! One person described rejection's nefarious side effects as: "It stinks and the smell is so strong, you can't even identify it." Many people have taken their own lives after they were rejected.

Some examples of great women and men

There is not a single person alive or dead who hasn't faced rejection once or twice. Some women were rejected by their fathers, even though they were still in mother's womb. They claimed that they weren't responsible for the pregnancy. Some regret this decision later.

Although there are many reckless men who enjoy sleeping with women today, they refuse to take any responsibility. To avoid having to assume responsibility for taking care of the baby and the woman they were pregnant with, these men will often deny it.

1

Rejection is a common phenomenon. This happens across borders and between countries. They may be rejected for their lack or origin of education. Other people might be rejected because their class, creed, and even their colour. Many are subject to rejection due to one or the other reason. People view you as someone who doesn't belong because they think you lack the ability to belong. Many people will turn down you because of the things you don't have. Sometimes they also reject you because of the things you have. The word of God tells me that rich people tend to have many friends. But poor people avoid having any friends. Low status means that some people will not answer their calls and won't want to have anything to do or talk with you. If you are successful, more people will want to identify with and support you.

Even God faces rejection

God has to face rejection. God loves everyone, and He desires for all to know Him. Some people don't believe in God. Others do not believe in God. Some call themselves atheists. These people believe that they are free thinkers, so they question the existence of an authentic God. He can govern the world and do whatever He wants. We are sure that they know this because of their ignorance and pretensions against reality. Even though they're in difficulty, these people will still call God even when they have bad news or strange things to report.

Joseph Stalin, one of the most ardent followers of Lenin. Karl Max was the father and founder of Russian revolution and socialism. However, before his death, he was so afraid of God that he had twelve rooms. According to his story, Stalin would move from one room to the other because of fear after sleeping in one place for 30 minutes. He died shortly after, but it is reported that he had said "O Nazarene," which was a reference to Jesus the Nazarene. Jesus must have appeared invariably to him. Everyone longs for the divine.

2

Everyone longs to be with the Almighty.

While we understand that some people may believe in God, they don't accept His sovereignty over their lives. Their view of the word God is a collection man's ideas. They do not believe that God has the right to rule their lives, but God is God and can never be moved. Even if we preach Jesus Christ until eternity, some will not believe the gospel. Some are afraid of their parents, religious leaders, or simply because of their hard hearts. The word of God declares that it is God's will that all men be saved and come to the knowledge the truth.

In 1987, I was part of a revival program in a church. One man, a Muslim blind man, lost his sight. He gave his life to Jesus Christ. He returned to his family and religious leaders, but they made him turn around. They said that he would never be a Christian since he was a faithful Muslim. He succumbed to their demands, and within a matter of minutes he was again blind. He sent us to him in the Church, and I was one among the brothers that was assigned to go and pray daily for him. He was deceived from the beginning. Because I stopped going back to his place for the prayers, I was unsure if he ever recovered. The word of God declares categorically

"My people have been destroyed by lack of knowledge. I will reject knowledge ...."" (Hos.4.6) God also stated that they would be rejected if they reject Him.

Many people only pay attention to the works of God. They have no respect for His ways. Many people suffer and languish in one or more of the problems they don't understand God's ways.

3

They will choose to die or to suffer hardship rather than to enjoy the freedom God's word has to offer. Many people today are miracle-seekers. Their goal is to find cheap miracles, or magical powers that one powerful man can conjure.

However, they aren't ready to learn the word or put it into practice. God stated that He will reject those who refuse His knowledge. God's word says

"Therefore, my people are taken into captivity because of their lack of knowledge; and their honourablemen are famished, their multitudes dried up from thirst." (Is.5-13).

Ignorance is worse than ignorance. It kills faster that any other deadly disease you could ever imagine. The truth of God's word cannot be a true deliverance. This is why so many people make a living making products of others.

"A hypocrite destroys his neighbor with his mouth; but, knowledge will deliver the righteous." (Pro.11.9)

The word of God tells you that you will find the truth, and that the truth will set your free. The knowledge of God's word will help you to know the truth and end your struggle.

Deliverance is not something you can do by running helter-skelter. Most people seeking deliverance today return home with more burdens, more demons. If you are willing to listen to God's word, you can end every demonic influence on your life. Although it's okay for a pastor or minister to pray for your needs, the pastor who lives by God's word should do so. Jesus Christ is described in the Bible as:

4

"When the night came, they brought many that were possessed of devils to Him; and he cast them out with his word and healed all that were sick." Matthew 8:16

I was informed that churches may charge registration fees for delivering people. Others will ask you to regularly visit their offices for checkups. This is spiritual witchcraft, to subjugate the people and enslave them. Only knowledge is able to set you free. You don't need to look for someone who can prophesy in your life. The word of God will guide you through your problems. Your life will change if you become a Bible believer and a Word-based church. You will soon see the change you want.

5

Chapter 23: Jesus was Rejected

Apart from the fact many people have rejected Jesus, there are many Sadducces who were Pharisees or Sadducces back in Jesus' day and also those who did not accept him as their Lord/Savoiur. It was considered blasphemy among religious leaders, chief priests and heads of synagogues when Jesus claimed to be the Son of God. Many saw Him as just another moral or ordinary person.

One day, I was on a trip with a friend in Maryland U.S.A. from Atlanta Georgia to Houston Texas. While we were flying on delta airlines, we were also on our way to Houston Texas. We met a Jew from Israel and decided to share the Gospel. Surprisingly though, she was hostile to us. Jesus was only her brother. Jesus was just an ordinary person to her. And this is what many Jew find today.

However, we recognize that Jesus is not a common or ordinary person. Jesus is not just a prophet as some mistakenly believe or believe. He is the messiah and the saviour sent by God to save the whole world. The father sent Jesus to the world out of love for us (Jn.3-16). The Bible states that He is the propitiation and atoning sacrifice for our sins as well as the sins for the whole of the world. (1Jn.2:2). Jesus is the way. No one can reach the father except through Him, according to the Bible. (Jn.14.6). The Bible also teaches that Jesus Christ is our only hope for salvation (Acts 4:12). The Bible says that Jesus Christ is the mediator between God & man.

"For there exists one God, and one mediator among God and men: the man Christ Jesus." (Tim.2 to 5) Through the amazing name of Jesus, we can pray and God will either answer or listen to us.

Do you see that? With all these obvious facts that are supported by scriptures that we won't be able to mention, many who reject Jesus for any reason whatsoever still reject him.

6

The Bible, as we all know, is the entire story of Jesus Christ.

His life is a series of events that runs from Genesis through Revelation. He is the seed for the woman in Genesis. He is also the Passover lamb in Exodus. In Leviticus, He is called the High priest. In Numbers, He is the Pillar for cloud by day and Pillar for light by night. Deuteronomy calls Him the prophet Moses, Joshua calls him the captain to our salvation. He is our judge as well as our lawgiver in Judges. He IS OUR Kinsman Redeemer in Ruth. In first and second Samuel He the trusted prophet. He is the King of the Chronicles. In Ezra he is the faithfulscribe. In Nehemiah he is the builder of the broken-down wall that separates human life. He is our Mordecai. In Job, He is the living redeemer. He is the shepherd of Psalms. He is also the wisdom of Ecclesiastes. In the Songs of Solomon he is our lover, and our weddinggroom. In Isaiah He is called the Prince of Peace.

He is the weeping priest in Lamentation. Ezekiel shows him as the remarkable four-faced man. Daniel portrays him as the fourth man to be baptized in the fire of life. Hosea He is the faithful husband. Joel He is a baptizer of the Holy Ghost fire. He is the bearer of burdens in Amos; in Obadiah He can save. Jonah describes Him as our great foreign missionary. Micah, on the other hand, is the one who is the messenger with beautiful hands. He is God's evangelist in Habbakuk and Nahum. He is our Saviour in Zephaniah. In Haggai, He is the restorer God's lost heritage. Zechariah says He is the fountain for sins and uncleanness in the house David.

Malachi, however, describes Him as the son of righteousness who rises with healing in His wings.

Mathew says He is the Messiah. Mark calls him the wonder-worker. Luke says He is the man's son; John says He is God's son. Acts says that He is the Holy Ghost. Romans describes Him as our Justifier. In the first and the second Corinthians, He is our sanctifier. In Galatians, He redeems us from the curse of law. Philippians identifies Him as the God that supplies all of our needs. Colossians reveals He is the Godhead who is bodily the fullness.

7

In First and 2nd Thessalonians, He is our King soon; in 1st and 2nd Timothy, He the Faithful pastor; and in Philemon He the beloved brother.

Hebrews calls Him the Blood of an everlasting covenant. James calls him the great physician. He is the chief shepherd and bishop of our soul in First and 2nd Peter. He is love, in First, Second and Third John. Jude depicts the Lord Jesus as He comes with ten thousand saints. In Revelation, he is the King and Lord of lords.

He is Abel's sacrifice. He is Noah's ransom. Hezekiah's sun dial. Daniel's burden. Malachi's sunof righteousness. He is Peter and Stephen's shadows, Stephen and Stephen's signs & wonders, Paul's handkerchief & apron, John and John's pearly white cities.

He is the husband of the widower, the father of the fatherless. He is the bright, morning star for the traveler by night. He is the bread that gives life to the hungry. To those who walk in lonely valleys He is the lily and rose of Sharon, the honey on the rock and the rose of Sharon for them. He is God's brightness; He is God himself.

He is the pearl for great price. He's the rock in weary lands, the cup overflowing, the rod and staff that comfort. He is Jesus Christ the Nazareth, and some ignorant ones reject Him. It is not possible to expect anything else if they reject Him. The same way his father sent him was how he sent them to us.

8

Jesus Christ is the focus of this discussion.

"He is despised by men and rejected by them; a man of sorrows, acquainted with grief; and it was our face from him; he wasn't respected and we do not respect him. Although he has borne our pain and carried our sorrows, we didn't think he was worthy of our respect. He was afflicted by God and was stricken. But he suffered for our transgressions; he was bruised by our iniquities; the chastisement to our peace was upon his shoulder and with his stripes, we are healed." (Isaiah53:3-5).

It is absurd to ignore Jesus and all He did for humanity. Some people detested Jesus so much, they said that he had Beelzebub. This is the prince demons. Jesus told them that a home divided against itself can't stand and that it was impossible for Him to cast out demons through the power demons. Jesus spoke these words of himself, and what will happen in his last days.

"For just as the lightning that shineth from one part of the earth, shineth to the other, so shall the sons of man be in their days." He will first have to suffer many hardships and be rejected by his generation. (Luke 17:24-25)

To put it another way, before He shined forth He was rejected. And that prophecy was fulfilled. Even His disciples rejected Him. Judas trampled Him, Peter denied

Him and Thomas refused to believe Him. Pilate also condemned Him. Summary: He is still everything God created Him to be, regardless of how many people reject Him. Rejection from people didn't change His assignment. Rejection didn't shift His focus. It could not hinder His success and the greatness God had for him. Jesus' rejection and His greatness and unmatched success are both described in the Bible.

9 781774 858981